I0190130

Paperback Quarterly

*"Journal of the
American Paperback Institute"*

CONTENTS

The Pecan Valley Press
Brownwood, Texas

PAPERBACK QUARTERLY features articles and notes dealing with every type (mystery, detective, science fiction, western, adventure, etc.) and with every aspect of new, old and rare paperbacks.

Emphasis is placed on the historical research of paperbacks, their authors, illustrators, publishers and distributors; but the editors also invite contributions of bibliographical interest. In short, the only criterion for the editors' consideration is that the subject matter pertain to paperbacks.

PQ pays ½¢ per word (200-4,000 words) for articles and notes. Payment on acceptance.

PQ is published in Spring, Summer, Fall and Winter of each year with a subscription rate of $6.00 per year or individual copies for $2.00 each. Institutional and library subscriptions are $8.00. Overseas rate is $12.00. All back issues are currently out of print.

All correspondence, articles, notes, queries, ads and subscriptions should be sent to 1710 Vincent Street, Brownwood, Texas 76801. (915) 643-1182.

Published & Edited by
Charlotte Laughlin   Billy C. Lee

Contributing Editors
Bill Crider   Thomas Bonn

Printer & Technical Advisor
Martin E. Gottschalk

Cover Logo Designer
Peter Manesis

Letters

Dear Editor,

I read Mark Schaffer's "A Glance at Paperback History" in the summer 1979 issue of PAPERBACK QUARTERLY and was immediately stung into action by his opening remark in paragraph 2 - 'For all intents and purposes, the modern paperback era began in 1939, when Robert DeGraff launched Pocketbooks, Inc.'

May I correct Mr. Schaffer by saying that at least on this side of the Atlantic the paperback made its debut on 30 July 1935.

I can do no better than ask the Editor kindly to reprint the story of Penguin Books which I have obtained from the Publisher.

Eric Tucker
Surrey, England

[The above letter was inadvertently left out of the last issue. See "The Penguin Story" in the Fall 1979 issue, page 18]

Dear Bill Crider:

Coincidence, coincidence...The volume 2, number 1 edition of PAPERBACK QUARTERLY lists Bruno Fischer's MURDER IN THE RAW as a 1957 Gold Medal book. My MURDER IN THE RAW came out in 1955, which you list in vol 2, #2.

After they bought THE BAD SAMARITAN, I sent a few chapters and a resumé in for the option try at Harlequin - and they have accepted that much and will pay the first half of the advance. If they buy it, it will be called (my title, so might be changed) THE CANA DIVERSION - Callahan again.

Thanks for the publicity.

Sincerely,
Bill Gault

[Next issue, we will hear more about Superior Reprint and Flagship Books]

The Saint Mystery Library
by M.C. Hill

Hats off to Leslie Charteris for his selecting the many great stories written by the greats in their field and acting in his capacity as editor and seeing produced THE SAINT MYSTERY LIBRARY series. This series is one of the most challenging to assemble primarily because the series is now nearing 20 years since conception which places most of them on the endangered specie list; as each year passes they become more difficult to locate.

On a 7,000 mile junket this last spring, we traveled through 10 north central states. I managed in two months time to meet over 300 book store proprietors and closely examine their stocks looking for the many scarce series but especially the Saint series. On arriving home and after sorting and checking through my many purchases I found that I had managed to pick up eight of the titles plus six duplicates of the eight. Geographically this does not mean that these items will not be found in quantities in other sections of the country as the vageries of accumulations and the collecting habits of readers varies from one section of the country to another. I find that I have no trouble locating stories by Eugene Manlove Rhodes when scouting in New Mexico. I also find that in cities with over 100,000 population, there are generally 10 or more used book stores where many of the scarcer series of mystery, detective books can be located.

Getting back to the series -- the main reason that this series is so valuable is the fact that among the 54 stories are 11 or more authors that have reached the pinnacle of success. No one doubts that Harlan Ellison is one of the most controversial writers to come on the scene in the past

20 years. His works are avidly sought out by
thousands of collectors who think nothing of lay-
ing out $5-$25 for some early story that appeared
in a 25¢ issue. One of his original stories,
"Find One Cuckaboo," appears in LET HER KILL
HERSELF (Saint Mystery Library #128).

All 14 books were produced by Great American
Publications, Inc. New York, New York. The first
six books #118-123 measure 4¼ by 6½ inches. The
remaining eight books #124-131 measure 4¼ by
7 1/8th inches.

The following is my estimation of their scar-
city by demand and availability: #121,120,122,123,
126,128,129,130,131,118,119,124,127,125.

John Jakes who has written many science fiction stories has also entered into other fields.
He appears six times in this series and all six
stories are originals. He hit it big in 1976 when
his seven volume Bi-centenniel series by Pyramid
appeared and was followed by a major television
series on the same theme.

E.E. Hoch appears twice in the series. He
brought into existence the now famous Simon Ark
(supernatural detective). One of these stories,
"City OF Brass," was reprinted later by Leisure
Books for which there is a big demand. Check
Ellery Queen Mystery Magazine(Feb. 1979) for one
of his most recent stories.

Fredric Brown appears twice in the series.
In my estimation he is one of the most popular
writers who ever wrote in both the mystery and the
science fiction field. Many of his stories are out
of print and are avidly sought by an ever growing
number of people all over the world.

Cornell Woolrich, August Derleth, L.G.
Blochman, Craig Rice, Poul Anderson, Baynard
Kendrick, Rufus King, Judith Merrill, Stewart
Sterling, Leslie Ford, Carl Jacobi, Richard Deming,
Hal Ellson, Frank Kane, Wenzell Brown, A.S. Roche,
Maysie Greig, H. Howard, J.E. Gunn, L.V. Ramos,
W. Oursler, I.E. Cox, G. Eliot, J. Stephens,

I. Thorne, R. Shahani, L. Whipper and R. Andrew are all represented at least once.

The Saint Mystery Library was really a mystery magazine in the form of a pocket-sized book, usually featuring one long story or novel and several short stories. Volumes in the series appeared from August 1959 until March 1960. The following is a complete list of the entire series.

#118   STAIRWAY TO MURDER by R. King (cover story)
       "The Very Groovy Corpse" by C. Rice
       "Walk Up To Fear" by M. Greig
       "Bad And Dangerous" by H. Ellson
       "The Amateur Assassin" by H. Howard
All five stories appeared in The Saint Mystery Magazine during 1956-58. The cover painting is by "Sussman." (August 1959)

#119   WITNESS TO DEATH by W. Brown (cover story)
       "A Package For Mr. Big" by F. Kane
       "For The Good Of The City" by A.S. Roche
       "City In The Bottle" by H. Howard
       "I Want It Fool Proof" by R. Deming
All five stories appeared
in the Saint Mystery Magazine during 1956-59. The
cover painting is by
"Sussman." (August 1959)

#120   MURDER SET TO MUSIC
       by F. Brown (cover
       story)
       "Corpse In A Suit
         Of Armor" by
         P. Anderson
       "Pill Roller" by
         J.E. Gunn
       "Open All Night
         by L.G. Blochman
       "The Eleven Diplo-
         mats" by J. Jakes

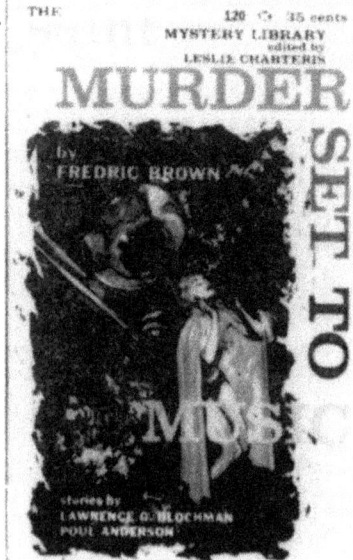

THE   120 ⊙ 35 cents
                 MYSTERY LIBRARY
                     edited by
                  LESLIE CHARTERIS
MURDER
by
FREDRIC BROWN
                              SET TO

MUSIC
stories by
LAWRENCE G. BLOCHMAN
POUL ANDERSON

6

All five stories appeared in The Saint Mystery
Magazine (except the J. Jakes story which is an
original) during 1956-57. The cover painting is
by "Sussman." (September 1959)

#121   THE FRIGHTENED MILLIONAIRE by C. Rice (cover
       story)
       "City Of Brass" by E.E. Hoch
       "The Nine Quilty Nannies" by J. Jakes
THE FRIGHTENED MILLIONAIRE appeared in The Saint
Mystery Magazine in 1956. The Hoch and Jakes
stories are originals. The cover painting is by
Ted Coconis. (September 1959)

#122   MURDER MADE IN MOSCOW by B. Kendrick (cover
       story)
       "Sign Of The Thunderbolt" by L.G. Blochman
       "Adventures Of The Little Hangman" by
         A. Derleth
       "The Legation Cigar" by C. Jacobi
       "Lunatic's Dictionary" by L.V. Ramos
       "The Honest Fakirs" by J. Jakes

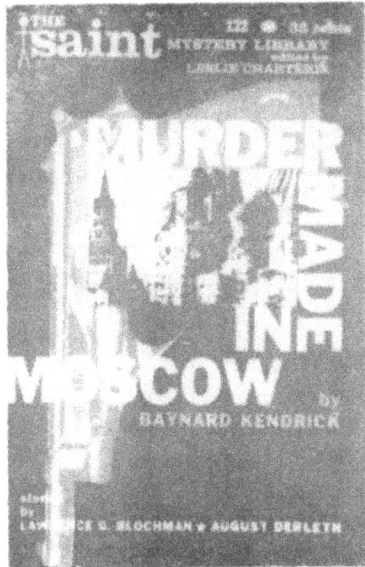

The first four stories appeared in The Saint
Mystery Magazine during 1957. The Ramos and Jakes
stories are originals. The cover painting is by
Luszcz. (October 1959)

#123   MURDER IN THE FAMILY by C. Rice (cover story)
       "Beast Of Prey" by T. Powell
       "Ceremony Slightly Delayed" by B. Traven
       "The Raised Dollar" by J. Trumball
       "The Dead Dodos" by J. Jakes
       "A Filipino 'FBI'" by H.S. Singh
"Beast Of Prey" and "The Dead Dodos" are original
stories. The other four appeared in The Saint
Mystery Magazine during 1954, 1957-59. The cover
photo is by Bob Ritta. (October 1959)

#124   DEATH STOPS AT A TOURIST CAMP by L. Ford
       (cover story)
       "Hula Homicide" by W. Oursler
       "The Big Deal" by S. Sterling
       "I Came To Kill" by I.E. Cox
"The Big Deal" and "Hula Homicide" originally
appeared in Private Eye for July 1953. The other
two stories appeared in The Saint Mystery Magazine
during 1954-55. The cover
photo is by G. Bellance.
(December 1959)

#125 RED SNOW AT DARJEELING
       by L.G. Blochman
       The cover photo is by
       Sid Miller.

#126 EXECUTIONER'S SIGNA-
       TURE by G.F. Eliot
       (cover story)
       "Vengeance" by J.
          Stephens
       "Miss Clarisa And
          The Grand Duchess
          by I. Thorpe

8

"Flame At Twilight" by E.E. Hoch
"Bud Of Paradise" by R. Shahani
THE EXECUTIONER'S SIGNATURE appeared in The Saint
Mystery Magazine for May 1957. "Vengeance" origin-
ally appeared in the July 1953 issue of Private Eye.
The other three are original stories. The cover
painting is by Frank Kalin. (January 1960)

#127 MURDER SEEKS AN AGENT by W. Brown
       Copyright 1945 by Mystery house
The cover painting is by G. Bellanca. (January 1960)

#128 LET HER KILL HERSELF by R. King (cover story)
       "Find One Cuckaboo" by H. Ellison
       "This Above All" by L. Whipper
       "Ten Lost Bombs" by J. Jakes
       "Dry Dust" by J. Merril
LET HER KILL HERSELF appeared in The Saint Detective Magazine, May 1956. "Dry Dust" appeared in
Double Action Western, February 1948. The remaining three stories are originals. The cover painting is by Frank Kalin. (February 1960)

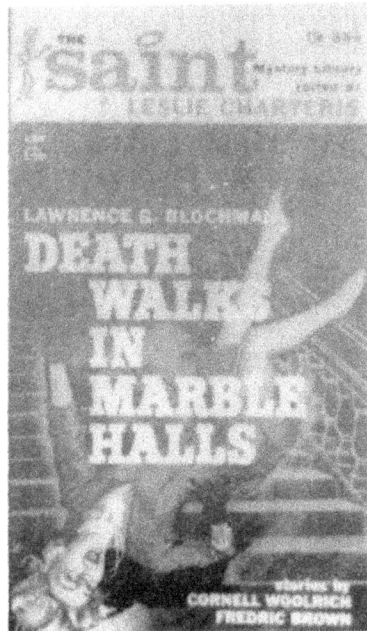

#129 INNOCENT BYSTANDER by C. Rice
    Copyright 1949
    (February 1960)

#130 DEATH WALKS IN MARBLE HALLS by L.G. Blochman
    (cover story)
    "Premier Of Murder" by F. Brown
    "Mimic Murder" by C. Woolrich
    "Night Of Gaiety" by R. Andrea
    "The Seven New Saints" by J. Jakes
"Premier Of Murder" originally appeared in The
Saint Detective Magazine, May 1955. "Mimic
Murder" was originally published in Black Mask,
June 1937 and reprinted in The Saint Myserty
Magazine in July 1958. The remaining three stories
are originals. The cover painting is by Leonard
Goldberg. (March 1960)

#131 THE RUM AND COCA-COLA MURDERS by W. Brown
    (cover story)
    "Calypsonian" by S. Selvon
"Calypsonian" appeared in The Saint Mystery Magazine in January 1957. THE RUM AND COCA-COLA
MURDERS is an original story. The cover photo is
by Larry Gordon. (March 1960)

     Beginning with #122, each book has at least
one page of introduction by Leslie Charteris
(except for #131 which has a three-page study on
Calypso).
     I am indebted to Robert Williams and Tom
Lesser for their aid in compiling this article.

PQ NOW PAYS CASH FOR NOTES AND ARTICLES; SEE PAGE 2.

Spotlight

Ten North Frederick

Paperback promotion sometimes comes in unforeseen ways. Such is the case with John O'Hara's TEN NORTH FREDERICK. As the "Publishers' Weekly" ad reproduced here indicates, this 50¢ Bantam was on the best seller list for 32 weeks, was a National Book Award winner, and was scheduled to "be a major 1957 movie!." The ad further indicates that O'Hara's novel was to be "backed by top promotion and publicity from BANTAM BOOKS."

But one wonders if the publicity supplied by the Detroit and Cleveland police departments had more of an effect in promoting TEN NORTH FREDERICK. In mid-January of 1957, they banned the paperback. Bennett Cerf, a director of Bantam Books, said the "action by the two cities was an 'outrageous' attack on freedom of the press." When John O'Hara heard of the banning, he satirically remarked "I am surprised that the Detroit Police Department

can spare a single patrolman for literary duty."
The January 14, 1957 "Publishers' Weekly"
article in which this quotation appears explains
that at the time of the police banning, Detroit
was ranked third in the nation in murders committed
annually.

Oscar Dystel, then president of Bantam Books,
said, "As a publisher, I am content to leave the
acceptance of any book to the good judgment of the
American people. A book as distinguished as TEN
NORTH FREDERICK, which is available everywhere else
in the country, must not be denied to the people
of Detroit and Cleveland...We and other publishers
have fought similar cases in the courts and won.
We certainly have no intention of permitting
arbitrary censorship to restrict our publishing
program."

By coincidence, only a month later, the
Michigan State Supreme Court heard a test case
concerning book banning which involved Pocket Books
and Detroit. The State Supreme Court reversed a
1954 conviction for selling Pocket Book's THE DEVIL
RIDER by John H. Griffin. The court ruled that
Michigan's obscenity law was unconstitutional.

In March, the County Circuit Court ruled
in favor of Bantam Books and voided the Detroit
ban of TEN NORTH FREDERICK. However, the Detroit
Police Commissioner immediately issued a statement
that in spite of the court order, anyone selling
TEN NORTH FREDERICK would be arrested. After
Bantam authorized it's attorney to file an
application to cite the Police Commissioner for
contempt of court, the Commissioner reversed his
decision to continue banning TEN NORTH FREDERICK.

Ironically, the banning controversy publicised
the paperback edition of O'Hara's book far better
than any promotional campaign Bantam could have
planned. Needless to say, the book was a success.

Rex Stout in the Dell Mapbacks
by Bill Lyles

DOUBLE FOR DEATH #9, 1943[George A. Frederiksen]*;
 reprinted as #495, with a revised map, in 1951
 [Robert Stanley].
THE MOUNTAIN CAT MURDERS #28, 1943[Gerald Gregg]
 reprinted as #D252, without map, in December
 1958[Al Brule].
TOO MANY COOKS #45, May 1944[Gerald Gregg]; reprint-
 ed as #540, with a revised map, in 1951[Robert
 Stanley].
THE RED BULL #70, January 1945[Gerald Gregg].
THE BROKEN VASE #115, May 1946[Gerald Gregg]; re-
 printed as #674, with a revised map, in March
 1953[Carl Bobertz].
ALPHABET HICKS #146, Jan. 1947[George A Frederiksen].
THE HAND IN THE GLOVE #177, 1947[Gerald Gregg].
RED THREADS #235, 1948.
NOT QUITE DEAD ENOUGH #267, 1948[Gerald Gregg].
BAD FOR BUSINESS #299, April 1949[Gerald Gregg].
3 DOORS TO DEATH #626, 1952[Rafael de Soto] (One
 of the 3 stories appeared as DOOR TO DEATH, 10¢
 book #21, without a map). *[] denotes illustrator.

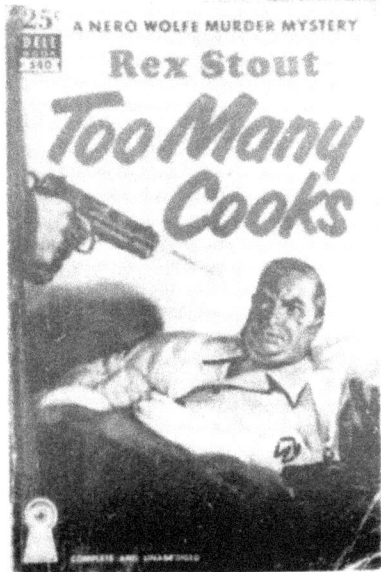

TOO MANY COOKS, Dell #45 & #540

Only four of these eleven Rex Stout mapbacks featured Nero Wolfe (#45,70,267,626); the others had the comparatively unexciting Tecumseh Fox (#9,115,299), the very dull Tyler Dillon (#28), the oddly-named Alphabet Hicks (#146), the fascinating female sleuth Dol Bonner (#177), and Inspector Cramer (#235). And none of the four Wolfe titles depicted Wolfe's house -- although William S. Baring-Gould has a ground floor plan in his NERO WOLFE OF WEST THIRTY-FIFTH STREET (Bantam #S4887, February 1970, p. 178). Dell editors and artists chose instead to show scenes they thought central to the books.

Both Dell editions of TOO MANY COOKS use maps

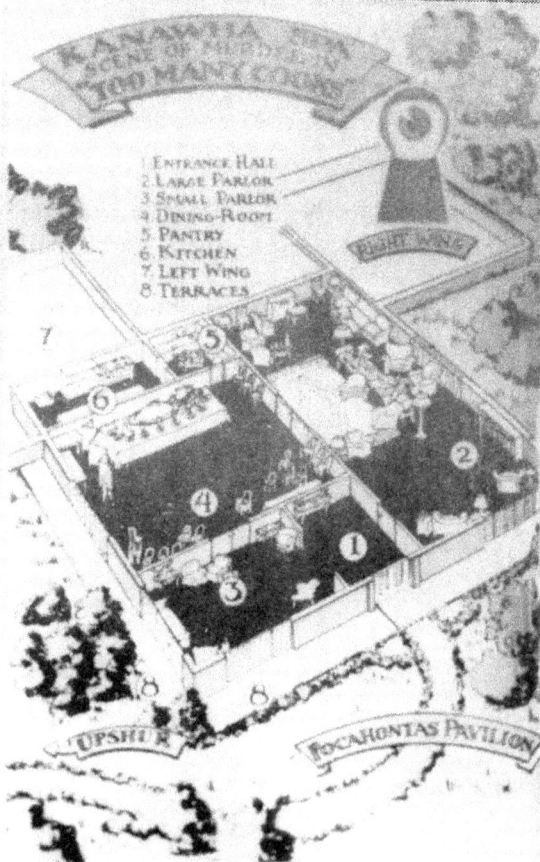

TOO MANY COOKS, Dell #45 mapback

(or diagrams) of Pocahontas Pavilion at Kanawha
Spa in Marlin County, West Virginia, where Wolfe
and others come for a massive feast. Both books
feature cutaway views of the pavilion interior,
#45 from the front, #540 from the right. The
latter edition (shown below) presents more detail,
more accurately perhaps, but #45 is much more
striking visually, its colors brighter, its black
floor in sharp contrast to the interior furniture.
As a small piece of evidence for the detail some
anonymous Dell Staff artist felt necessary, con-
sider the nine dishes of squid prepared for the
taste-contest, the nine cards before the dishes,
the water pitcher, the electric server, the plates

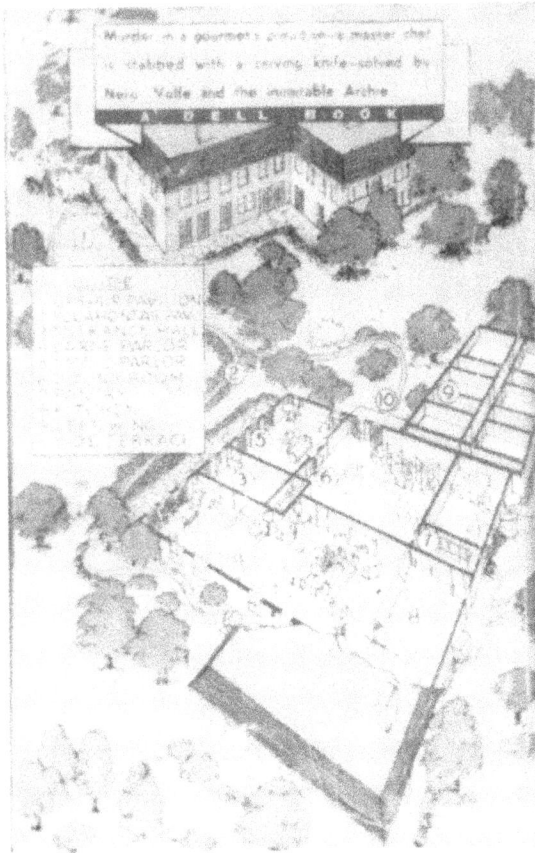

TOO MANY COOKS, Dell #540 mapback

THE RED BULL
Dell #70 mapback

and forks -- all visible,
if microscopically, in the
dining room. Both maps
are excellent additions
to a fine Nero Wolfe opus,
maps that I think make
these Dell editions su-
perior to other paperback
editions. (Unfortunately,
Dell omitted the recipes
from #45, however.)

THE RED BULL adopts
a view of Thomas Pratt's
farm in upstate New York.
The view is pleasant,
though hardly necessary
to understand the plot,
even if a few details
don't correspond to Stout's
descriptions -- the too-
small garage (p. 17), for
example. Too Bad the

NOT QUITE DEAD ENOUGH, Dell #267

3 DOORS TO DEATH, Dell #626

artist didn't picture Wolfe sitting and stewing
atop the boulder in the pasture, but Dell rarely
showed people -- alive or dead -- in the maps.
I believe they felt that such representations
would give away too much of the plot. (Note:
The Dell edition of THE RED BULL is slightly
abridged, unfortunately.)

NOT QUITE DEAD ENOUGH contains the title
story and "Booby Trap"; the map of 316 Barnum
Street in New York City, with a cutaway view of
Miss Leeds' Apt., illustrates the former story.
A much better choice would have been a map of
Nero Wolfe's apartment to illustrate "Booby Trap."

3 DOORS TO DEATH presents, as part of the
second-generation Dell maps, three views of the
interiors central to the stories: the 12th-story
showroom at dressmakers Daumey & Nieder, 496
Seventh Avenue, New York City, for "Man Alive";
the reception hall of Mrs. Floyd Whitten's townhouse,

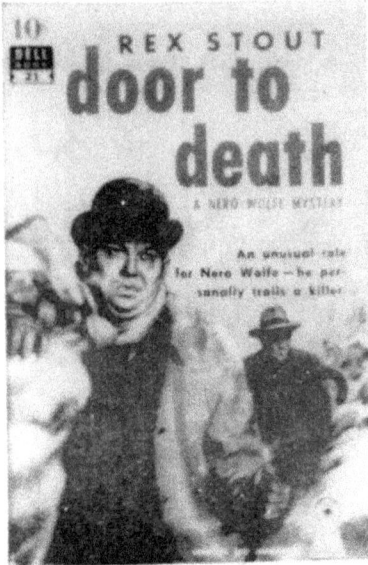

DOOR TO DEATH
Dell 10¢er #21

in the East Seventies between Fifth and Madison, New York City, for "Omit Flowers"; and Joseph G. Pitcairn's country house in the village of Katonah, northern Westchester county, N.Y., for "Door to Death." None are particularly striking, although in the artist's defense Stout gives little detail of the three locales.

The first Dell edition of DOUBLE FOR DEATH features an elaborate overhead view of Maple Hill, the country estate in Westchester county, plus

DOUBLE FOR DEATH, Dell #9

18

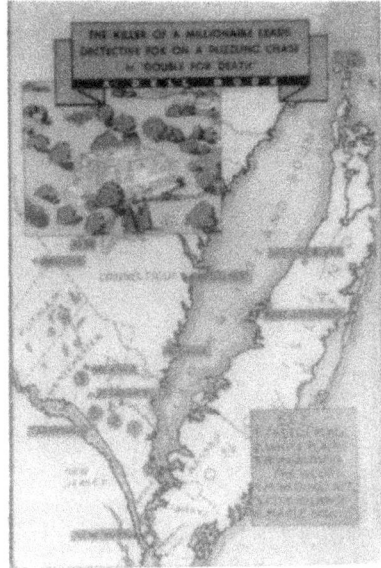

DOUBLE FOR DEATH, Dell #495

THE BROKEN VASE
Dell #115 mapback

a small inset of the country. The second Dell edition reverses the order, unfortunately, leaving the reader with an unnecessarily large view of the county and a meagre view of the estate. Much of the detail of Maple Hill was filled in by the artist, yet the reader can still easily follow Tecumseh Fox's walks around the estate (pages 135-136 and 144-146, for instance). The cutaway interior of the house is lovingly and painstakingly detailed, from porte-cochere to music

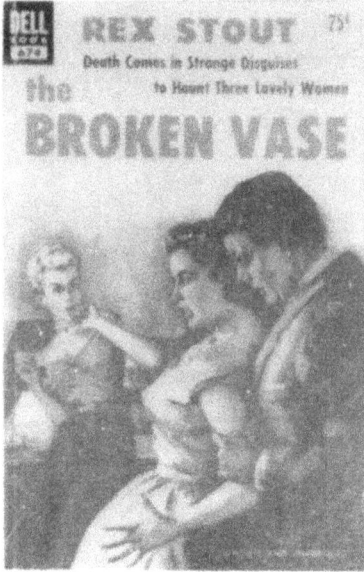

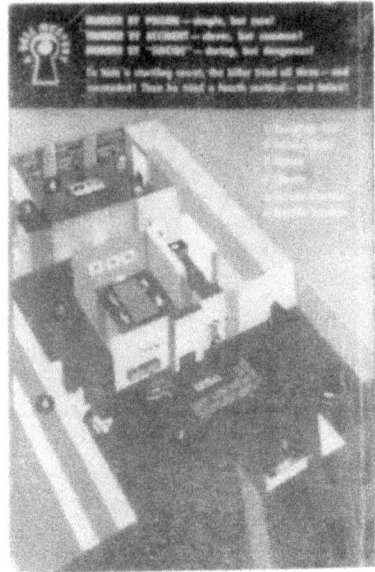

THE BROKEN VASE, Dell #674

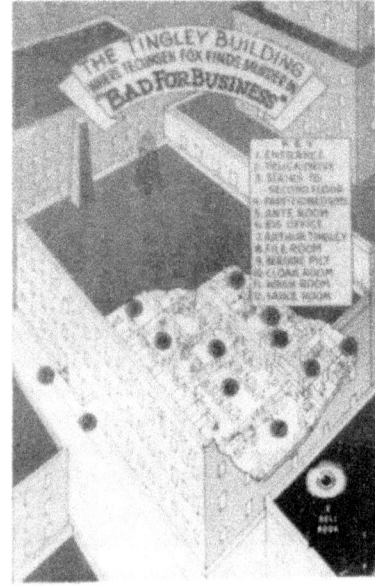

BAD FOR BUSINESS, Dell #299

room.

THE BROKEN VASE has a beautifully detailed
view of Henry and Irene Pomfret's apartment on
the 20th floor of 3070 Park Avenue, New York City--
on the first Dell edition that is; the second is
a colorful but bare copy. The Yellow Room with
two pianos, the dining room and library with purple
floors don't exactly correspond to the book's details, true, but the book is dull, anyway. The
map is much better.

BAD FOR BUSINESS features a fairly good map,
one that must have given the artist some trouble,
since Stout's descriptions of the Tingley Building
(home of Tingley Tidbits, appetizers; at Twenty-
Sixth Street and Tenth Avenue, New York City) are

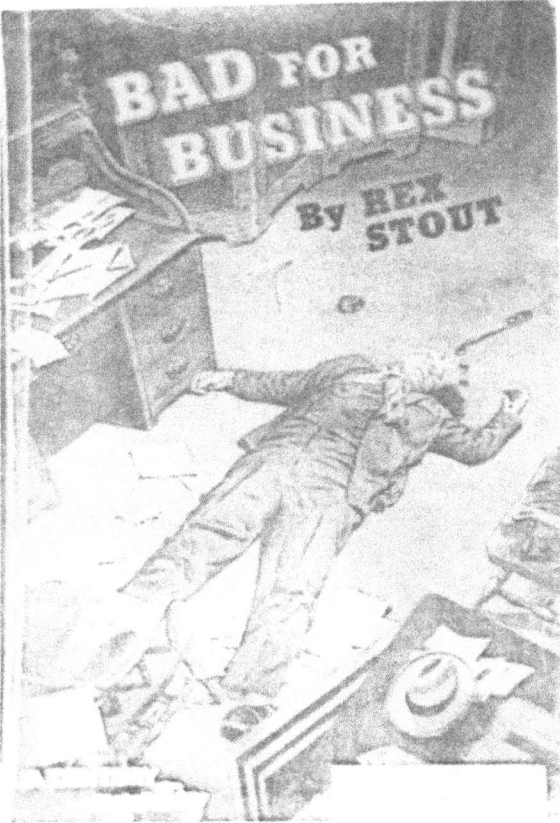

BAD FOR BUSINESS, Century

21

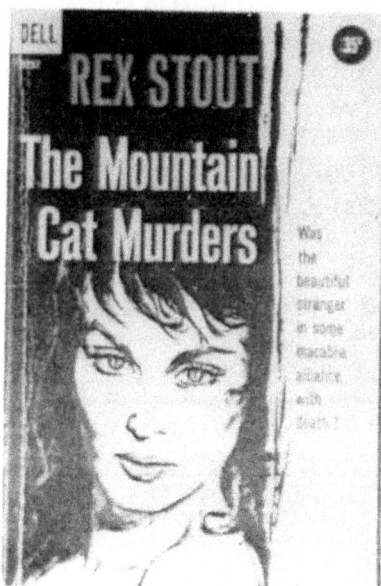
THE MOUNTAIN CAT MURDERS
Dell #D252

a bit confusing. A better idea might have been to split the map: half Tingley's office, half New York City. The front cover of the Century digest-sized edition #28, but the way, pictures a detail of Tingley's office, very detailed, with Tingley's corpse. (Note to sticklers: the folding screen is placed correctly on the Century cover, not so on the Dell.)

The map of the Old Sammis Building on Halley Street in Cody, Wyoming on THE MOUNTAIN CAT MURDERS is beautifully garish, its reds, yellows, and greens eye-boggling.

THE MOUNTAIN CAT MURDERS, Dell #28

ALPHABET HICKS, Dell #146

THE HAND IN THE GLOVE, Dell #177

And the detail is accurate down to the spittoons
in Dan Jackson's office. Interesting that Dell
should feature such a bright map on a book with
such dark psychological undercurrents.

The map on ALPHABET HICKS is mislabeled: it
should read "R.I. Dundee Laboratory" (in Westchester county), not "R.I. Dundee & Co. Factory."
But the details are well arranged, even though the
map doesn't extend to the orchard and Crescent
Farm, both of which are important in the book. The
titular character is, like A.A. Fair's Donald Lam,
a disbarred lawyer, but not half as interesting.
But the map is fun.

THE HAND IN THE GLOVE has a map of Birchhaven,
the country estate of Peter Lewis Storrs near
Ogowoc, Conn. Considering the mass of detail Stout
gives us, I think the artist has done a remarkable
job of synthesis and placement. (Country estates
are usually more difficult to draw from authors'
descriptions than diagrams of houses or apartment

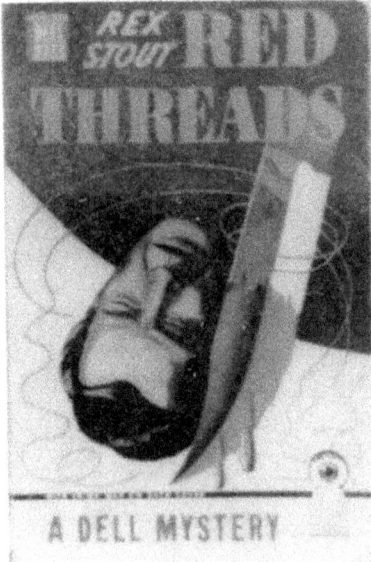

RED THREADS, Dell #235

24

interiors, obviously. Or is it obvious?) The vegetable garden might be more detailed, and the table is misplaced, but the map remains a fascinating complement to Rex Stout's most interesting non-Wolfe novel. (See pages 171-176 for a very strange marriage proposal.)

RED THREADS features the only tomb in the Dell mapback series: that of Tsianina Carew, on the Carew estate at Mount Kisco in (where else?) Westchester county. Other views of the tomb appear on the front covers of the Pyramid Green Door edition (R-1098; repeated, smaller, on Pyramid R-1373) and on the extremely scarce Los Angeles Bantam #A1 (which, like the Dell edition, was produced by Western Printing & Lithographing).

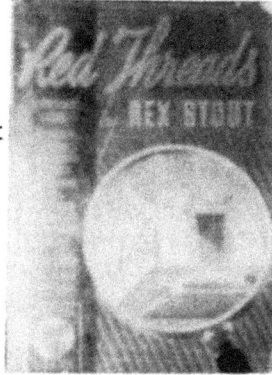

RED THREADS
Bantam LA #A1

Again, how unfortunate that Dell didn't have a complete set of Nero Wolfe mapbacks. But those Rex Stout titles it did produce make colorful and pleasant collectible paperbacks.

----In the future, I might examine the mapback editions of other authors: Agatha Christie (17 books with maps), A.A. Fair (10), Leslie Ford (7; and 1 as David Frome), Delano Ames (3), John Dickson Carr/Carter Dickson (11), Edgar Rice Burroughs (2), Matthew Head (5), and Brett Halliday (a zillion). I'm open to other suggestions.

Bill Lyles
77 High Street
Greenfield, MA 01301

25

The Bonibooks
by Peter Manesis

In talking to friends who want some explanation of the mania that covers my study's walls, I always find it difficult to pinpoint the beginning of paperbacks as a phenomenon. Often as not I pick out LOST HORIZONS, hand it over, and say that it was the first one. I used to start to qualify that, but people don't like complications; they want to see a first one, hold it, say yes that is well made, then head back to the card table, having sufficiently humored me.

Well, so much for them. As you and I know, there were all sorts of paperbacks before the paperbacks. In 1939, Pocketbooks just sort of distilled 200 years of sporadic experiments and came up with a combination of marketing and format that was exactly right for the times. No single feature was new.

Most of the stuff that came before was so short-lived that it could barely fill a shelf, or so generally boring that no one would want to go to the bother. With the cavalier disregard of the newcomer, I passed up a lot of the pre-paperbacks during my first year or two of collecting. The 40s, I was convinced, were it.

Then while I was pouring through some odds and ends in a local shop one afternoon, the dealer asked if I'd ever seen or was interested in BONIBOOKS. No, I hadn't, but let's take a look. By the immutable law that governs such things, it was irretrievably buried, so I'd have to check back later.

The next day I didn't have to ask. Lying on the counter, I just sensed that that was it. I picked it up and ....hmmm. Signature bound, oversized, great heft (like the early Pockets), nice art deco wraparound cover, absolutely gorgeous endpapers (Rockwell Kent?!), and in the back a partial list of 20-30 others!

26

That was enough -- I was hooked and the chase
was on.

OK, so hold it. These aren't Avons. No
electric covers or bondage babes. If your taste
runs strictly to high gloss and 50s flashart, skip
the rest of this.

The BONIS are really not like anything else
you've come across and, inasmuch, reflect their
creators, publishing renegades Charles and Albert
Boni. Having lost the firm of Boni and Liveright
to Liveright on a coin toss, the brothers, looking
for something to do, cooked up the idea of selling
cheap, attractive reprints via subscription. They
got Rockwell Kent to come up with cover and endpaper formats, then pushed out a sample edition of
Thornton Wilder's then immensely popular BRIDGE OF
SAN LUIS REY. Interest ran hot enough and in June
1929, the PAPERBOOKS were born.

It's not clear if the line bombed or if the
Boni boys got starry-eyed, but within a year or so
they scrapped the subscription idea and went to
selling outright through bookstores (50¢ each)
under the new name BONIBOOKS. The 16 titles which
had appeared as PAPERBACKS would eventually be re-
issued under the new imprint, the final number of
which reached at least 43.

The BONI and PAPERBOOKS are alternately ex-
citing and exasperating from the collector's
standpoint. It's the kind of line that will let
you down, then pick you up again. Just when you've
sworn off waiting around the mailbox to unwrap another routine cover, a perfect gem will turn up and
get you hooked all over again. For sure, it will
get on your nerves seeing the same half dozen titles
offered repeatedly on booklists. But to the die-
hard, that sort of thing serves only to steel
resolve and keep the fires burning.

It's not that they are that hard to find. In
less than three years I've unearthed more than half
of them, so they are around. For one thing, booksellers tend to hang onto them because they look

PAPERBOOKS

BONIBOOKS

PROSPERITY FACT or MYTH
☆ STUART CHASE ☆

Charles Boni PAPER BOOKS *New York*

The Return of the
HERO
DARRELL FIGGIS

Charles Boni PAPER BOOKS *New York*

The Master of the Day of Judgment
LEO PERUTZ

Charles Boni PAPER BOOKS *New York*

PAPER BOOKS

WANDERING WORLD

Above and Below: Two of Kent's endpaper designs.

CRIME AND DESTINY
JOHANNES LANGE

INTRODUCTION BY
J.B.S. HALDANE

Charles Boni PAPER BOOKS *New York*

classy and feature a lot of rarely reprinted, out of the way literature, much of it surprisingly radical.

Unpredictability, throughout, is the keynote. One title showed up in no less than an illustrated paper slipcase, which gives rise to no end of idle speculation. And if your fetish runs to variants, you can have a field day here since color combinations were sometimes overhauled from one printing of a title to the next, yielding covers that are at once the same and different.

By 1932 the BONIBOOK experiment succumbed to the Depression, to remain but another interesting sidepath in the evolution of the paperbacks. The Boni brothers, themselves, would go on to other visionary projects, not the least of which was a home library of microprinted books. Probably the one thing they could not foresee, however, was that 50 years down the line a breed of well-intentioned eccentrics would be scouring through the sale bins trying to piece together the heiroglyphs of a story long forgotten.

Happy hunting!

**The editors of Paperback Quarterly
are saddened to learn of the death of
Howard Waterhouse**

Book Sellers

The following people sell paperbacks by mail. Most mail out booklists on a regular basis and all are knowledgeable paperback collectors.

WILLIAM & PAT LYLES
77 High St.
Greenfield, MA 01301
(413) 774-2432

MICHAEL BARSON
Bowling Green English Dept.
Bowling Green, OH 43403
(419) 255-9305   WSA#389

VIVA BOOKS
365 E. Cuyahoga Falls Ave.
Akron, OH 44310

JEFF PATTON
3621 Carolina St., N.W.
Massillon, OH 44646

JUDY K. REYNOLDS
9969 B Sloanes Sq.
St. Louis, MO 63134
(314) 429-6654

ED KALB
3227 E. Enid Ave.
Mesa, Arizona 85204
(602) 830-1855

GRAVESEND BOOKS
Box 235
Poconopines, PA 18350
(717) 646-3317

McCLINTOCK BOOKS
P.O. BOX 3111
Warren, OH 44485
(216) 399-7348

THE LEFT HAND OF DARKNESS
Jan Landau
441 Ford St. #8
West Conshohocken, PA
19428

HOWARD WATERHOUSE
P.O. BOX 167
West Upton, MA 01587
(617) 529-3703

BUNKER BOOKS
P.O. BOX 1638
Spring Valley, CA 92077
(714) 469-3296

STEVE LEWIS
62 Chestnut Rd.
Newington, CT 06111

JEFF MEYERSON
50 First Place
Brooklyn, NY 11231

PAPERBACK PARADISE
468 Centre St.
Jamaica Plain, MA 02130

JACK IRWIN
16 Gloucester Lane
Trenton, N.J.08618

BARRY & WALLY PATTENGILL
Rt. 3 Box 508
Waco, Texas 76708

Paperback Bodies
by Bill Crider

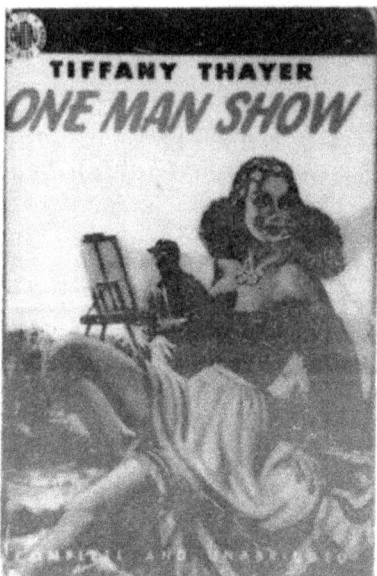

After the first novelty of paperback books wore off and hundreds of different titles began competing for newsstand space, something had to be done to insure sales of books which were not already guaranteed them (hardcover best sellers could be expected to sell well) and to attract attention to a particular title and help it sell even better than it might ordinarily be expected to do. No one should be surprised that the one thing used to do this was sex. The covers of the books were what potential customers saw on the

stands, and the covers got the treatment. One gathers that most of the customers were men, because it seems that the majority of paperback covers feature pictures of women in various states of undress exhibiting various portions of their invariably shapely anatomies.

BOSOMS

Let's face it, one of the most outstanding examples of anatomy exposed on covers is

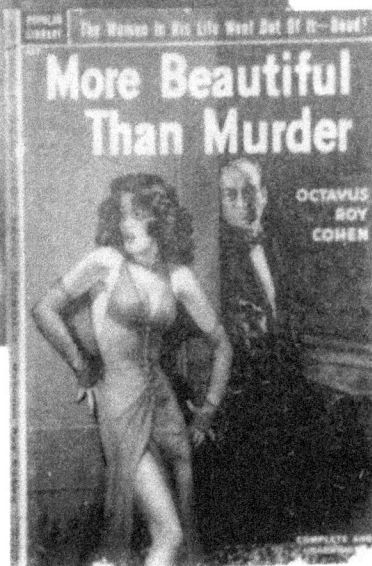

breasts. The cover of W. Somerset Maugham's THE GENTLEMAN IN THE PARLOR (Avon #147, 1947) leaves little doubt as to why the "gentleman" is so interested in the lady who occupies the central position. A little sadism added to the sex never hurts, as the cover of MURDER HAS MANY FACES (Graphic # 105, 1955) indicates. There's not much showing, but the threat is certainly there, as it is in THE CAPTAIN'S LADY (Popular Library

#266, 1950) where the woman bears a marked resemblance to Maureen O'Hara. And what better threat than a few noble savages dancing around a hapless maiden as on the cover of SAVAGE CAVALIER

(Popular Library #G104, 1952), where we are told that "She Traded Her Body For Her Life." Another nice example is the cover of ONE MAN SHOW (Avon # 327, 1951), which features a nice pair of legs as well. And we should at least point out the over-emphasis made by some illustrators regarding the female anatomy. Covers like on Raymond Chandler's FINGER MAN (Avon #219, 1950) show us what dressing styles the public considered popular in the

34

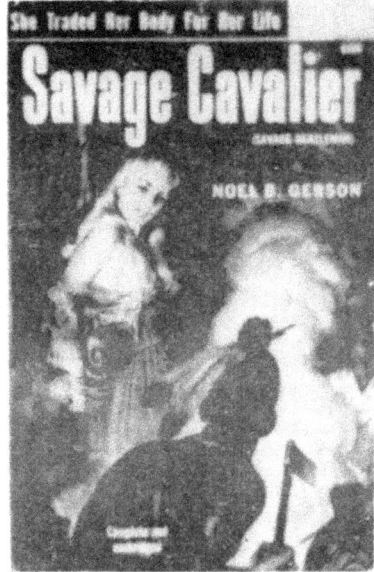

1950s. (Did I say point?)
And this section wouldn't be
complete if we didn't men-
tion the all time favorite,
GENTLEMEN PREFER BLONDES
(Popular Library #221, 1949).
It's the depth the illus-
trator uses which makes
this classic cover popular
among collecters. The en-
ticing blonde in the fore-
ground and the goggle-eyed
men in the background say
it all.

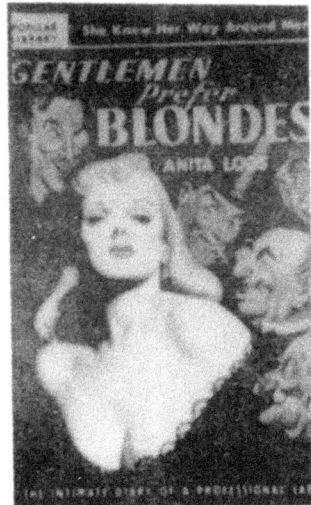

LEGS
      Leg men are in for more
than their share of delight when studying the
merits of old paperback covers. Dell was never
noted for sexy covers, but a couple of hardboiled
mysteries feature gorgeous gams: ARMCHAIR IN HELL
(Dell #316, 1949) doesn't show a chair, but it

does show part of a woman who must be adjusting her stockings; and the wonderfully straight seams on GIVE 'EM THE AX (Dell #460, 1950) extend from an early version of the miniskirt. Ace's 1960 DEAD CERTAIN gives us legs in black and white, while Graphic's 1953 DARK DESTINY shows clearly what short shorts are all about. Forget the dead man; who's looking at him? After all, he's fully dressed. Not so on most dead women, as the cover

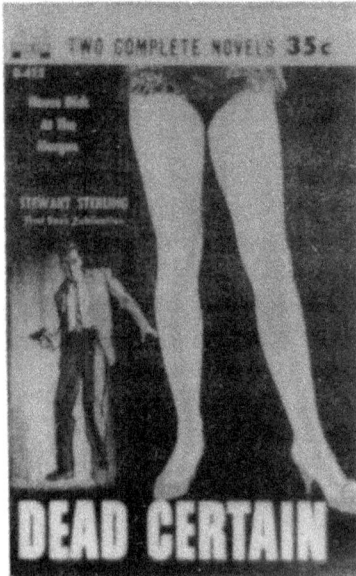

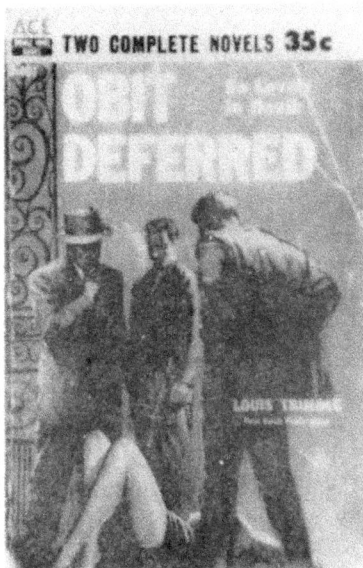

FLIGHT INTO TERROR
(Signet #1378, 1955)
reveals. Women always
die in dishabille on
paperback covers. OBIT
DEFERRED (Ace #D401,
1959) is another example
as is LOVELY LADY, PITY
ME (Avon #282, 1951).

BACKS
    If you are more
into the peekaboo look,
you might prefer the
many covers which give
you a good look at a
woman's back, with a
hint that much more is
to be seen if you just
hang around. A fine example is THE GO GIRLS
(Monarch #330, 1963). Need any help with that
zipper, miss? FRAMED IN BLOOD (Dell #578, 1952)

gives us a back and a
little front at the
same time, while THE
LAST NIGHT (Gold Medal
#909, 1959) and STRANGER
IN PARIS (Bantam #423,
1949) pick up the same
motif. Those robes
are just about ready
to fall, as is the dress
on THE SURFSIDE CAPER
(Ace #505, 1961). TWO
HOT TO HANDLE (Paperback
Library#52-233, 1963)
and THE DOCTOR'S WOMAN
(Avon#817, 1958) give
us not only some very
good backs but a couple
of fine bottoms as well.

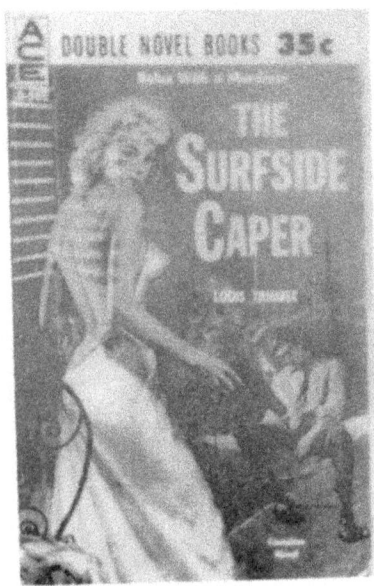

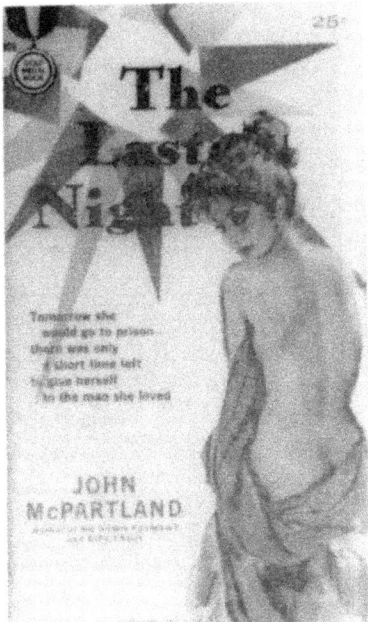

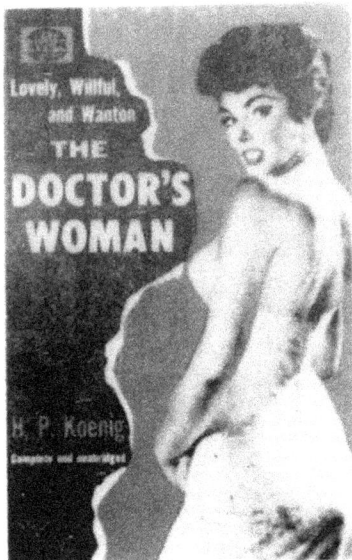

FIVE ALARM FUNERAL
(Dell #816, 1954) gives
us another one of those
dead lovlies, a jacket
discreetly thrown across
her midsection, with
back and legs exposed.

THE WHOLE THING

How do artists
manage to get in a whole
body, clothed but sug-
gestive? Well, they can
give the girl a really
great, if outrageous,
dress, like the one on
MORE BEAUTIFUL THAN
MURDER (Popular Library
#427, 1952) or the one
on THE LEATHER PUSHERS
(Popular Library #288,
1950). Or they can do a

39

THE
LEATHER PUSHERS

HE WAS A PUSHOVER FOR A DAME

A great ring classic by one of
the world's great humorists

H. C. WITWER

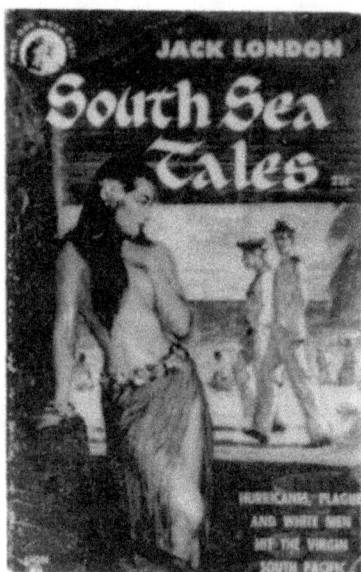

JACK LONDON

South Sea
Tales

HURRICANE, PLAGUE
AND WHITE MEN
HIT THE VIRGIN
SOUTH PACIFIC

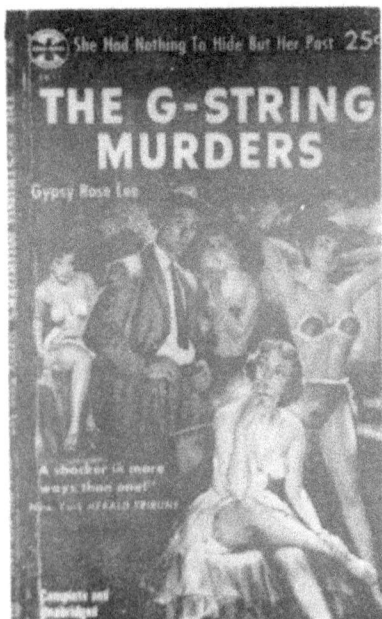

She Had Nothing To Hide But Her Past 25¢

THE G-STRING
MURDERS

Gypsy Rose Lee

A shocker in more
ways than one!
New York HERALD TRIBUNE

Complete and
Unabridged

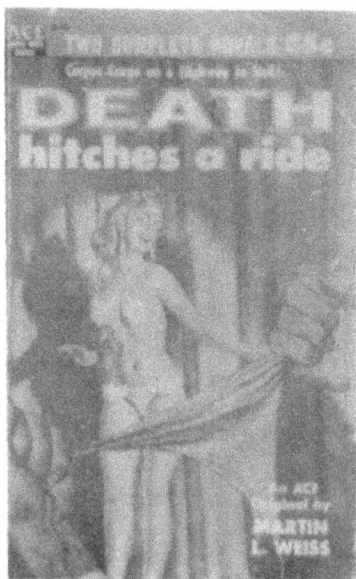

DEATH
hitches a ride

an ACE
novel by
MARTIN
L. WEISS

native girl to illustrate
SOUTH SEA TALES (Lion #92,
1952). Or they can do
strippers, which fit
naturally with THE G-STRING
MURDERS (Popular Library
#EB15,1954), and well, if
not naturally, on DEATH
HITCHES A RIDE (Ace #D45,
1954). Or they can give
us the female at bay, in
another of those great
dresses, like the one on
LINE ON GINGER (Avon #333,
1951). Or, finally, they
can give us just a
straightforward naked
woman in bed, as on DIE,
LOVER (Avon #T450, 1960).

Who knows whether the
exhibition of sexy poses
sold books? No one,
probably, but someone must
have believed it did,
because he gave us so
many of them.

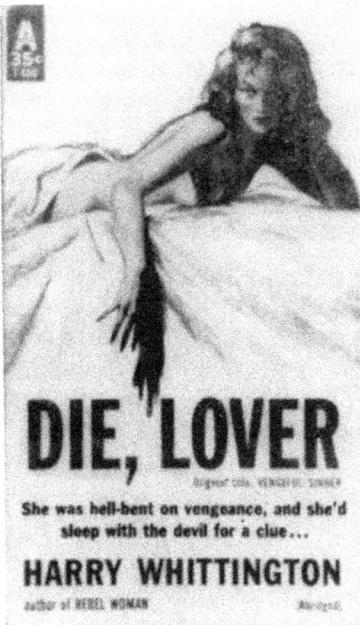

41

Selling Culture with Paperback Covers
by Mark Schaffer

The appeal of the paperback has many layers of popular culture appreciation. One of the most intriguing areas for me is the fascinating shotgun marriage of marketing, popular culture and serious art that inexpensive printings of major writers demand. Around the various paperback boardrooms the question of how can we sell a Henry Miller, a Celine, a Zola to a different audience has resulted in a curious spectrum of solutions. Let's look at some of these strategies to sell "culture" in the drugstore.

In important ways the earliest Pocketbooks of DeGraff in the late 1930's and 1940's were too tentative in their aesthetic purpose to make large distinctions between serious literature and more popular fiction, as can be seen by comparing Bronte's WUTHERING HEIGHTS (PB #7) and a typical adventure novel like Sabatini's CAPTAIN BLOOD (PB #38). Serious and middle brow were viewed simiarly in that respectable novelistic middle range graphic style. Some early Pocketbooks looked exactly like their hardbook counterpart. De Maupessant (PB #12), Jane Austin's PRIDE AND PREJUDICE (PB #63) and Jan Struthers' MRS. MINERVER (PB #159) are good examples. Pocketbooks was cautious about marketing serious literature to the read and run audience and their cultural choices reflect tellingly on 1930's tastes, which were largely Victorian

JAN STRUTHER

Parlor Room genteel: Austin, Hugo, Butler and Hardy. Modern American and continental writers don't begin to see reprint until the late 1940's, and these were chiefly Bantam's efforts (Hemingway, Fitzgerald, Twain).

Of course the war retarded much fiction reprinting along these lines. Yet, afterwards, only Bantam, Pocketbooks, Penguin and later Signet made concerted efforts at offering serious pocket literature besides the endless river of Spillanes, Runyans, Christies and their scores of followers.

From the Late 1940's through the early 1950's writers like D.H. Lawrence, Celine, Truman Capote, Gore Vidal, Aldous Huxley, George Orwell and others were exposed to a vast audience which was in some ways now prepared by the war, to confront these more ambiguous contemporary fictional visions. Here, however is where the story becomes more intriguing. Committed to selling serious work, the paperback publishers chose a strategy which compromised the form to achieve their goal. American paperback houses in the post-war years turned from the bold surrealism and expressionism of the war-time covers to the lurid, pulp style of naturalism represented on THE MALTESE FALCON and the more naturalistic Avati and Soyer-like realism of Signet's covers. With the transition to a distinct style, Celine, Huxley, and Orwell went into the marketing hopper right along with with Hammett, Sayers, Thorne Smith and Eric Ambler. Leaving aside the question of deceptive advertising

43

for the moment, let's observe some of the more charming results of this union of art and Madison Avenue.

Pocketbook's THE SCARLET LETTER (PB #551) depicts a dramatic confrontation between Hester Prynne and the old moralistic biddies of Salem in that high key lit Hollywood style; Avon sold Celine's JOURNEY TO THE END OF THE NIGHT (G1014) with an intense urban movie poster naturalism that was hight popular in the early 1950's, and in many ways misrepresented the French author's context, as did Bantam's ANTIC HAY (#1142, 1953) by Aldous Huxley. D.H. Lawrence was retooled by Berkley Medallion for THE WOMAN WHO RODE AWAY (G59), a preposterous jungle cover that, curiously enough, cuts through to Lawrence's primal core.

Other excellent examples of the trend include photographic-like war drama on Pocketbook's RED BADGE OF COURAGE (PB #154, 1949), a graphic DAY OF THE LOCUST (Bantam #1055, 1953), Gore Vidal's homosexual work THE CITY AND THE PILLAR (Signet #773, 1950) with Avati's characteristic moody

realism. It is interesting to note that this
novel of "gay" love features a woman prominently
on the cover. A favorite of mine in the movie
poster school of literature popular in the 1950's
is Bantam's ALL THE KINGS MEN (Bantam #939). This
great cover truly captures the smoked-filled,
grubby backroom world of Willy Stark, Robert Penn
Warren's unforgetable creation; and true to Bantam's
philosophy, there are more movie-like teaser scenes
on the back of the book. A great cover.
Fitzgerald went through several incarnations in the
late 1940's as three illustrations will attest.
The 1946 Bantam THE GREAT GATSBY (Bantam #8)
reflects the light, carefree, pleasure filled
ethos of his complex novel. In 1949, the movie
tie-in edition displayed a beefcake Alan Ladd in
a daring homoerotic cover scene. By 1951, however,
the cover had become more "civilized" and John
O'Hara'd. A separate study could be made on the
little teasers paperbacks merchants have placed on
covers to lure buyers. The 1951 "Gatsby" announces
"The famous novel of a man's ruthless drive to

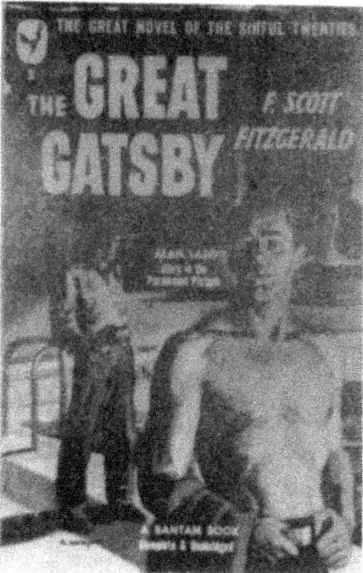

wealth-to buy back the haunting past." Try putting
that on a college term paper. Soon after,
Fitzgerald became a literary icon and respectable
art began to appear on his paperback reprints --
Permabooks' THE BEAUTIFUL AND THE DAMNED (Permabooks #123), heralding Fitzgerald's arrival in
the Pantheon. Hemingway underwent similar treatment. The 1949 THE SUN ALSO RISES (Bantam #717)
features a tense, shirtsleeved, movie-type Jake
Barnes, bottle at his elbow. The teaser delicately
asks "Could he live without the power to love?".
Fortunately the prose survives nicely. Inciden-
tally, Bantam frequently reprinted a small photo
of the original hardcover edition on the back of
its books. It is sobering to realize that
Hemingway was introduced to the world in the 1920's
with whimsical art noueau dust jackets. In 1954
Oscar Dystal, Bantam's new publisher, put a stop
to all this nonsense with a bold stroke. The 1954
THE SUN ALSO RISES featured a black and white
photograph of the bearded author and a long exposi-
tory blurb about Hemingway's legacy to the world
and literature. The "re-
lationships of men and
women" had, in four
years, replaced "love,"
signalling that the
1950's had really taken
over the paperback. By
this time it was too
late to go back to the
carnal sensuality of
Popular Library's
BURMESE DAYS (PL #459).
Soon the major paper-
back houses would de-
velop separate editions
for serious literature--
Bantam Classics, Dell
Laurel Editions, Signet
Classics. The pendulum

46

had swung the other way. Never again would
Lawrence be sold with a tawdry harlot in
dishabille. It was Vintage Press from now on
and the process continues. Only recently genre
writers like Raymond Chandler and James M. Cain
have attained the heights of trade reprintings,
following Dashiell Hammett. This is all leading
to a delicious irony in the business--after
selling serious art to the masses for years,
now the game is polishing the pop scribes for the
elite. And, if any trade publishers are reading
this, don't you think you've been dragging your
feet with Thorne Smith, Cornell Woolrich, and
John Collier? Don't be caught with your pants
down again.

As can be seen, the paperback is an endless
source of cultural insight into both the charming
logic of Madison Avenue and larger socioaesthetic
issues that have never really been addressed.
Perhaps this article will stimulate some new
directions of inquiry for PAPERBACK QUARTERLY
readers.

WILLIAM & PATRICIA LYLES
77 High Street
Greenfield, MA 01301

WANTS: Dell ALL-MYSTERY digest-sized book; ALL
WESTERN #3 (digest-size), Bantam #4,5,8,9,
10,12,14,15,95,97,98 (only with decorated
endpapers. Dell #23,51,57,58,60,61,71,83,
84 (with cellophane covers). Dell #63,70
(only copies with little numbers at the
upper left of the front cover and that don't
have cellophane on the covers). Especially
need Dell #767 DEAD MAN'S PLANS by Eberhart.
ALSO HAVE MANY PAPERBACKS FOR SALE. LIST #9 READY
SOON. SEND $1 FOR THE NEXT THREE LISTS.

Recent Releases

R. Reginald, editor, SCIENCE FICTION AND FANTASY
LITERATURE: A CHECKLIST, 1700-1974, WITH
"CONTEMPORARY SCIENCE FICTION AUTHORS II"
(Two volumes, Gale Research, 1979).

R. Reginald's SCIENCE FICTION AND FANTASY
LITERATURE can only be described as a monumental
work. Its first volume contains 15,884 entries,
each one a first edition of a book or pamphlet published between 1700 and 1974 in the fields of
science fiction, fantasy, and weird fiction. In
the first half of the book, listing is alphabetic-
ally by author; the book's title, publishing information, and format (cloth or paper) are given.
The second half of the volume is given over to a
title index, a series index, an awards index, and
even an Ace and Belmont Doubles index.
      The second volume consists of 1443 biographical
sketches of modern SF writers. Many of these are
brief and contain only basic information: name,
date and place of birth, personal and career data.
A fair number, however, also contain personal state-
ments by the authors, and most of these are quite
interesting (Samuel R. Delany has one which ques-
tions the validity of first editions of popular
fiction, for instance).
      It is impossible to convey, in a short review,
the amount of information contained in these two
volumes, and there's more. Volume II even has a
short pictorial history of science fiction. The
illustrations are wonderful, but (my only complaint)
in black and white. I'm sure that color would have
been far too costly.
      At $64 per set, these books are probably beyond
the reach of all but the most fanatical of collectors,
but now is the time to go to your local librarian
and give him/her the good word. Let's support
Reginald's fine work and dedication and see if we can
get these books into every library around.
                              --Bill Crider

John Nieminski, THE SAINT MAGAZINE INDEX (Cook &
    McDowell Publications, 1980)

   Indexing is a tedious, thankless job. Few
people have the nerve to attempt it; fewer still
are tenacious enough to stick to the task and do
it right. John Nieminski is one of the few, and
Cook & McDowell are to be congratulated for signing
him up to do a series of indexes of the entire
field of digest-sized mystery magazines. (John
has previously published EQMM 350, an index to the
first 350 issues of ELLERY QUEEN'S MYSTERY MAGAZINE.)
THE SAINT MAGAZINE INDEX is a meticulous alphabetical listing, by author and by title, of all material
published in all 141 issues of THE SAINT MAGAZINE.
Series characters are noted in the author listing,
and there is an alphabetical list of series characters given as an appendix. Alternate titles are
given in another appendix. All lists are cross
referenced. If you're interested in mystery writers
and their short stories, you've got to have this
book. If you're not interested and just love
lists, you need it. Or if you just take simple
pleasure in a job well done, you should order it.
(Just to whet your appetites for more, I'll add
that Nieminski is now working on an index to
ALFRED HITCHCOCK'S MYSTERY MAGAZINE, which I hope
will be the second in this series.)
   Copies of THE SAINT MAGAZINE INDEX are available for $6.75 (postage paid) from John Nieminski,
2498 Western, Park Forest, Illinois 60466. Or
from Cook & McDowell Publications, 3318 Wimberg
Avenue, Evansville, Indiana 47712.
                        --Bill Crider

Robert Egan, THE BOOKSTORE BOOK (Avon #46474, 1979)
    $5.95

   Since leaving New York City, I have had a
recurring dream: without warning I am given a huge

sum of money that must be completely spent on books in two days. (No money for shelving or storage, however. That as we know is a nightmare that follows!) To keep the books I must visit every bookstore in the city within 24 hours and make at least one purchase at each store, so I journey to Manhattan in a Hertz-Rent-a-Bookmobile. If I fail in my mission, books and bookmobile will self-destruct and all I will be left with is a stack of coverless Harlequin romances.

Next time I have this dream I can relax. I now have at hand Robert Egan's THE BOOKSTORE BOOK: A GUIDE TO MANHATTAN BOOKSELLERS. Egan has uncovered over 750 stores of all types, categorized and de-scribed them with annotations that list their lo-cation (including cross streets), phone numbers, hours, specialties, and peculiarities. The general categories of bookstores include remainder shops, used and antiquarian stores, as well as hundreds of stores under type and under subject heading. Auction galleries and out-of-print record shops are also listed. Egan anticipated the logistical problem of my fantasy and provides a breakdown of stores by geographic area within Manhattan and maps of these areas.

For paperback collectors who can visit Manhattan, the book is a must. Egan, an editor at Pocket Books, has provided under "Used Book Stores" a subsection, "Used Paperback Stores." Thirteen stores are listed, including six "exchange" stores that have cropped up in New York City over the last couple of years. In other sections, "used paperbacks" are noted for those stores that, while not specializing in old paperbacks, have large sections of them for sale.

A worthy addition to Bowker's AMERICAN BOOKTRADE DIRECTORY; better get a copy before the listings become dated and all your mapbacks turn into stripped Harlequins!

--Thomas Bonn

www.ingramcontent.com/pod-product-compliance
Lightning Source LLC
Chambersburg PA
CBHW021116020426
42331CB00004B/516